D0990834

SCIENCE BEHIND THE COLORS
MANDARINFISH

by Alicia Z. Klepeis

pogo

Ideas for Parents and Teachers

Pogo Books let children practice reading informational text while introducing them to nonfiction features such as headings, labels, sidebars, maps, and diagrams, as well as a table of contents, glossary, and index.

Carefully leveled text with a strong photo match offers early fluent readers the support they need to succeed.

Before Reading

- "Walk" through the book and point out the various nonfiction features. Ask the student what purpose each feature serves.
- Look at the glossary together. Read and discuss the words.

Read the Book

- Have the child read the book independently.
- Invite him or her to list questions that arise from reading.

After Reading

- Discuss the child's questions. Talk about how he or she might find answers to those questions.
- Prompt the child to think more. Ask: Did you know about mandarinfish before reading this book? What more would you like to learn about this fish?

Pogo Books are published by Jump!
5357 Penn Avenue South
Minneapolis, MN 55419
www.jumplibrary.com

Copyright © 2021 Jump!
International copyright reserved in all countries. No part of this book may be reproduced in any form without written permission from the publisher.

Library of Congress Cataloging-in-Publication Data

Names: Klepeis, Alicia, 1971- author.
Title: Mandarinfish / by Alicia Z. Klepeis.
Description: Pogo books edition.
Minneapolis, MN: Jump!, Inc., [2021]
Series: Science behind the colors | Includes index.
Audience: Ages 7-10 | Audience: Grades 2-3
Identifiers: LCCN 2020003635 (print)
LCCN 2020003636 (ebook)
ISBN 9781645275831 (hardback)
ISBN 9781645275848 (paperback)
ISBN 9781645275855 (ebook)
Subjects: LCSH: Dragonets—Juvenile literature.
Classification: LCC QL638.C15 K54 2021 (print)
LCC QL638.C15 (ebook) | DDC 597.5/7—dc23
LC record available at https://lccn.loc.gov/2020003635
LC ebook record available at https://lccn.loc.gov/2020003636

Editor: Jenna Gleisner
Designer: Molly Ballanger

Photo Credits: bluehand/Shutterstock, cover, 4, 23; stockpix4u/Shutterstock, 1 (top); arka38/Shutterstock, 1 (bottom); Dobermaraner/Shutterstock, 3; Mike Workman/Shutterstock, 5; Jnichanan/Shutterstock, 6-7; wildestanimal/Shutterstock, 8-9; Johannes Kornelius/Shutterstock, 10; Fenkie Sumolang/Dreamstime, 11; scubaluna/Shutterstock, 12-13; Vojce/Shutterstock, 14; Izanbar/Dreamstime, 15; Thomas Hasenberger/Shutterstock, 16-17; CK Ma/Shutterstock, 18-19; Erik Schlogl/Alamy, 20-21.

Printed in the United States of America at Corporate Graphics in North Mankato, Minnesota.

TABLE OF CONTENTS

CHAPTER 1
Flashy Fish 4

CHAPTER 2
Unique Patterns 10

CHAPTER 3
Impressing Mates 14

ACTIVITIES & TOOLS
Try This! 22
Glossary 23
Index 24
To Learn More 24

CHAPTER 1

FLASHY FISH

What fish has flashy colors and **patterns** and is shorter than a library card? This colorful creature is a mandarinfish! It is tiny. Adults are about three inches (7.6 centimeters) long.

coral

They are bottom-feeders. What does this mean? They stay near the bottom of the ocean. They look for food among the **coral reefs** where they live.

Coral reefs are home to small ocean creatures the fish eat. These include tiny worms and **crustaceans.**

TAKE A LOOK!

Where in the world do these fish live? Take a look!

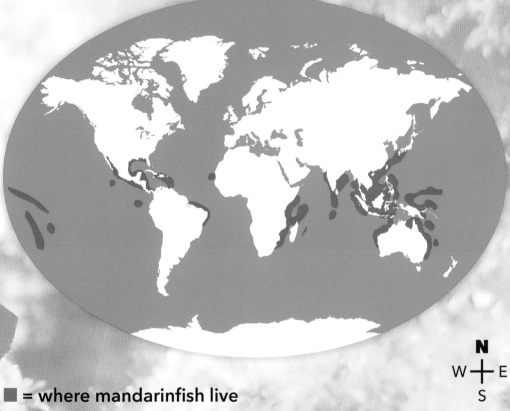

■ = where mandarinfish live

Mandarinfish have a unique way of swimming. They quickly **pulse** their pectoral fins. This allows them to **hover**. They can also use their pelvic fins to move along the ocean floor.

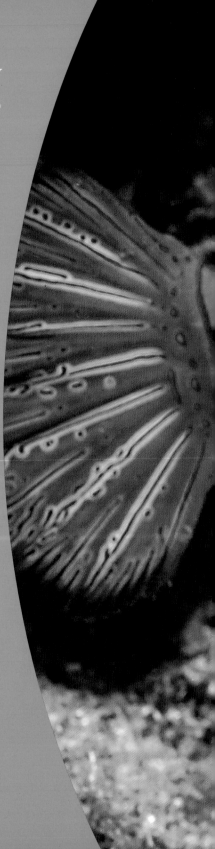

DID YOU KNOW?

You can tell female and male mandarinfish apart. How? Look at their dorsal fins. A male has a long, pointed dorsal fin. Female dorsal fins are shorter and round. Females are also smaller than males.

dorsal fin

pectoral fin

pelvic fin

CHAPTER 2

UNIQUE PATTERNS

Mandarinfish have patterns of wavy lines. They can be orange, red, yellow, or brown.

pattern

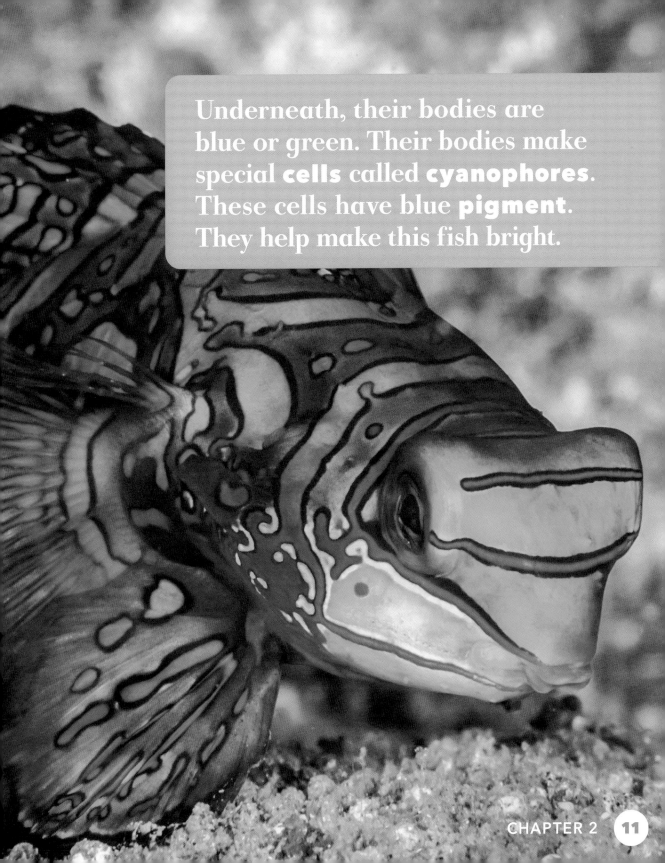

Underneath, their bodies are blue or green. Their bodies make special **cells** called **cyanophores**. These cells have blue **pigment**. They help make this fish bright.

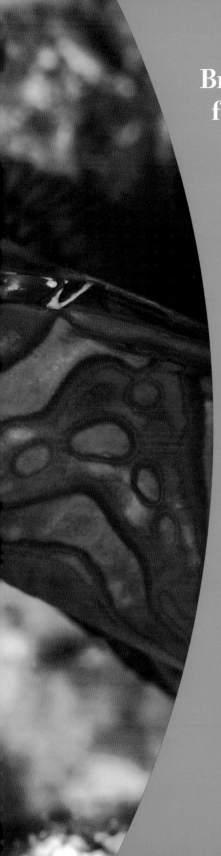

Bright colors help keep these fish alive. How? They warn **predators** to stay away. Mandarinfish do not have **scales**. Instead, a layer of **mucus** covers their skin. It tastes bad to predators that try to eat them.

DID YOU KNOW?

Mandarinfish often live in pairs or small groups. Their patterns are unique. No two look exactly the same!

CHAPTER 3

IMPRESSING MATES

Mandarinfish are normally shy. But they aren't shy when it comes time to **mate**.

Males try to **impress** females. Female mandarinfish choose bigger, brighter males as mates. Why? Brighter colors show that a fish is healthy. This also means the fish is good at finding food.

male

Once a female chooses a male, the pair swims higher in the ocean. They do a swim dance together and **spawn**.

young
mandarinfish

After the eggs hatch, the **larvae** are colorless. Very young mandarinfish are light brown. It does not take long for them to get their bold coloring. After just a few weeks, the patterns start to appear.

DID YOU KNOW?

Larvae are on their own from the start. Their parents do not have any parenting duties. Mandarinfish can live 10 to 15 years in the wild.

Mandarinfish are famous for their good looks. But their pretty patterns and crazy colors do more than dazzle. They warn predators and help attract mates. These fish are spectacular to see!

ACTIVITIES & TOOLS

WARNING COLORS AND PATTERNS

Mandarinfish aren't the only animals that warn predators with their colors or patterns. Research and create your own with this activity!

What You Need:
- sheets of paper
- colored pencils, crayons, or markers
- scissors
- large sheet of paper or poster board
- glue or tape

1. Using print or online sources, find at least four animals, not including mandarinfish, whose coloring or patterns work to warn predators. Some examples are skunks, bees, and monarch butterflies.

2. Print or draw examples of each. Note their distinct colors and patterns. Use scissors to cut out the pictures. Attach these examples or drawings to half of your poster board with glue or tape.

3. Imagine you have discovered a new animal that uses colors or patterns to scare away predators. Draw the animal in its habitat. Show its colors and patterns. Place this drawing on the other half of your poster board. Note the similarities and differences to the other animals you researched.

GLOSSARY

cells: The smallest units of animals and plants.

coral reefs: Long lines of coral that lie in warm, shallow waters.

crustaceans: Sea creatures with outer skeletons.

cyanophores: Special cells that have blue pigment and reflect light.

hover: To remain suspended in one place.

impress: To make someone or something feel admiration or respect.

larvae: The very early forms of an animal after hatching.

mate: To join together to produce babies.

mucus: A thick, slimy liquid produced by mucus membranes that can protect an animal.

patterns: Repeating arrangements of colors, shapes, or figures.

pigment: A substance that gives color to something.

predators: Animals that hunt other animals for food.

pulse: To beat or throb.

scales: The thin, flat, overlapping pieces of hard skin that cover the bodies of reptiles and fish.

spawn: To produce a large number of eggs.

INDEX

cells 11

colors 4, 13, 15, 19, 20

coral reefs 5, 6

crustaceans 6

cyanophores 11

dance 16

dorsal fins 8

eggs 19

female 8, 15, 16

hover 8

larvae 19

male 8, 15, 16

mate 14, 15, 20

mucus 13

ocean 5, 6, 8, 16

pairs 13, 16

patterns 4, 10, 13, 19, 20

pectoral fins 8

pelvic fins 8

pigment 11

predators 13, 20

spawn 16

swimming 8, 16

worms 6

TO LEARN MORE

Finding more information is as easy as 1, 2, 3.

1. Go to www.factsurfer.com
2. Enter "mandarinfish" into the search box.
3. Click the "Surf" button to see a list of websites.

FACT SURFER